Miss Piper's Playroom
Helping Wendel With His Worries

by Lynn Louise Wonders

Illustrated by Uliana Barabash

Wonders Counseling Services, LLC
Wonders Counseling & Consulting

Jacksonville, FL
United States

©2022 Copyright by Lynn Louise Wonders. All Rights Reserved

Printed in the United States of America

1st Edition

Visit Wonders Counseling & Consultation at

www.WondersCounseling.com

For Madeline

Hi! I'm Miss Piper!
Welcome to my playroom!

When children and families are having hard times in life at home, school or work.... when their feelings feel just TOO BIG to handle, coming to visit me in my playroom for a while can help them feel better.

I want to introduce you to Wendel. Wendel's mother brought him to meet me because Wendel had a lot of worries. SO many worries, in fact, that they were causing Wendel to have a lot of problems at home and school.

Wendel was even worried about meeting me for the first time and about being in a strange, new place.

Wendel's worries were SO big that Wendel couldn't feel happy to see all the fun things in my playroom.

All Wendel could do was stand in the middle of the playroom with his hands stuffed in his pockets.

I invited Wendel to sit with me. Together we quietly looked around the playroom. Then... I had an idea!

"Wendel, would you like to help me build a tower with my blocks?"

"Okay..."

While Wendel and I built a tower together, I wondered what kinds of worries Wendel had fluttering around inside of him, causing him problems.

After we built the tower, I invited Wendel to join me at my creative art table.

"MY TUMMY HURTS A LOT. IS THAT BECAUSE I HAVE A LOT OF WORRIES?"

"SOMEONE ONCE TAUGHT ME THAT WORRIES ARE KIND OF LIKE BUTTERFLIES IN MY TUMMY... NOT REAL BUTTERFLIES OF COURSE! BUT BIG, FLUTTERING FEELINGS INSIDE THAT MAKE MY STOMACH HURT SOMETIMES!"

"HMMM... SOUNDS LIKE YOU'RE THINKING ABOUT HOW YOU MIGHT HAVE WORRY BUTTERFLIES TOO!"

Together, Wendel and I cut out some paper butterflies. I invited Wendel to write on the butterfiles what kinds of worry thoughts he had that might be fluttering around inside, bothering him and causing problems.

Wendel had lots of worries. He worried about a lot of things.
Wendel worried that bad things might happen.

My mom might forget to pick me up

Our house might catch fire

I migt forget to turn in my homework

I might get really sick

My dog might run away

Wendel's mother brought him to see me again the next week. Wendel was still feeling a lot of worried feelings. It takes time to feel better. I knew that Wendel had come to the right place! In time, all those big worries would become lighter and smaller.

Another time in the playroom, Wendel and I played a game called Boss The Bubbles!
Wendel pretended the bubbles were his worries.

Wendel popped and stomped the bubbles.

He batted them and blew them around the room.

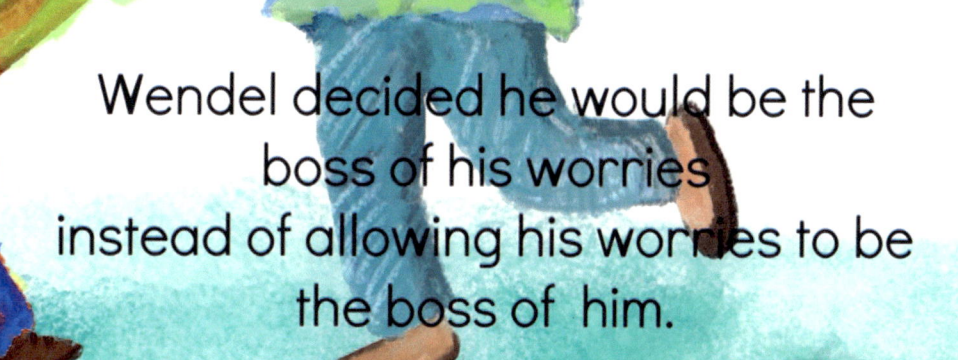

Wendel decided he would be the boss of his worries
instead of allowing his worries to be the boss of him.

After Wendel came to see me in my playroom many more times, he started feeling better. He smiled more. He laughed more. Wendel's worries were getting smaller.

As Wendel's worries got smaller, Wendel's mother and father joined Wendel and I in the playroom for family games.

Wendel's parents learned some fun ways to help Wendel keep his worries small and his happy feelings big.

After Wendel's worries stayed very small and after Wendel and I spent many therapy sessions playing together, Wendel and I noticed how many things in his life were better! Wendel was smiling and laughing more.

Wendel's school work became easier and Wendel even felt brave enough to learn how to ride a bike!

Wendel was able to go to new places with a happy hop in his step!

It was time for us to say goodbye. Wendel chose to draw a picture of himself for me to keep so I could remember our play times together.

Like Wendel, you can help your worries become smaller and lighter so you can do more things and have more fun!

Thank you for visiting my playroom! Bye bye!

Therapist's Corner . . .

Often children with generalized anxiety are so overwhelmed with worries that it's helpful to use some structured and directive play-based and creative-expressive activities to facilitate awareness, empowerment and mastery.

Resources and Ideas:

1. Even when introducing directive activities, always remain child-centered in your attunement to the child's body language, facial expressions and actions using authentically communicated tracking and reflection statements.
2. Always greet the child and parents with a very warm welcome. You want to establish the playroom as a safe and fun place to be.
3. Building towers together can serve as a metaphor for the process of therapy. Sometimes it is fun! Sometimes it is challenging. Sometimes we feel anxious during therapy but together we can work and play together.
4. Based on an intervention from Liana Lowenstein (many helpful books at www.lianalowenstein.com), the Butterflies in My Tummy intervention helps children become aware of the somatic signs of anxiety and it also helps children to name their worries so the child can join in the process of developing a plan with goals for the therapy.
5. Boss The Bubbles is an intervention that uses fun, big-body movement to help discharge the anxiety, help with regulation and empower the child to use his power of choice for focusing thoughts.
6. Be invitational! Invite the child to explore your sand tray or your sensory station.
7. Paris Goodyear-Brown has another useful book called The Worry Wars in which you'll find stories and additional interventions.
8. For a collection of fun, breathing activities and self-regulating coloring, check out my book called BREATHE for children and their caring adults available on Amazon.

Look for MORE books in the Miss Piper's Playroom Series!

Introducing Children to the Playroom
Separation Anxiety
Grief & Loss
Moving to a New House or School
Divorce
ADHD
Autism
AND MORE!

About the Author

Lynn Louise Wonders has been supporting children and families in the playroom and therapy office since 2002. She is licensed and certified as a professional counselor-supervisor and registered as a play therapist-supervisor. Ms. Wonders enjoys teaching therapists about the power of play in support of children and families. She loves creating books for children and adults to help them with their processes of growing, learning and healing. She is the author of **When Parents Are at War: A Child Therapist's Guide to Navigating High Conflict Divorce & Custody Cases** available on Amazon.

You can learn more about Ms. Wonders' work at WondersCounseling.com

Made in the USA
Columbia, SC
03 July 2024